The United States Constitution

Study Guide

ISBN 0-9635364-3-5

Second Edition

December 1996

Academic Solutions, Inc.
1520 West Warner Road
Suite 106-171
Gilbert, AZ 85233

Notice from the Editor

The statements and other information in this book are presented with the understanding that the publisher and the authors are supplying general information for broad educational purposes only. Due to the changing and complex nature of the subject matter of this text, the publisher and author cannot guaranty the accuracy of the information contained in this work, and the user acknowledges that the publisher and editor are not responsible for any such inaccuracies.

Table Of Contents

The United States Government can be accessed on the World Wide Web at:

http://www.whitehouse.gov/

This web site includes links to the many executive departments and agencies, the House of Representatives and Senate, the Supreme Court, and many other government sites. By beginning browsing at this site you can easily find many interesting information resources of the U.S. Government. You can also send the President E-Mail.

Table Of Contents

[illegible]

The Declaration of Independence — Study Guide

The Revolutionary War began in April of 1775. The British attacked colonial militias in Massachusetts. On June 7, 1776, Richard Henry Lee of Virginia made a proposal in the Continental Congress. He said that the colonies should be free and independent states. On June 10, 1776, a committee was appointed to write a declaration supporting Lee's proposal. The committee members included John Adams, Benjamin Franklin, Thomas Jefferson, Roger Sherman and Robert Livingston.

Thomas Jefferson was chosen to write the Declaration. On July 2, 1776, delegates from twelve of the colonies voted and approved Lee's resolution. On July 4, 1776, the final version of the Declaration of Independence was adopted by the Continental Congress. The public first heard the words of the Declaration on July 8, 1776. The actual Declaration of Independence was signed by John Hancock and forty-nine other members of Congress on August 2, 1776.

The Declaration of Independence

Preamble

On July 4, 1776, in Congress, the thirteen states unanimously made this declaration.

Sometimes it becomes necessary for a group of people to separate from a country and form their own nation. When this happens, the reasons for this separation should be explained.

Human Rights Statement

We believe the following truths are clear and obvious. We believe all people are created equal. We believe our creator gives each of us certain rights that cannot be taken away. We believe that included in these rights are the right to life, liberty, and the pursuit of happiness.

To make sure that the people have these rights, governments are formed. Governments get their power from the people they govern.

If any government takes the peoples' rights, the people have the right to change or abolish that government. The people may form a new government. The basis for this new government should be the safety and happiness of the people. Governments should not be changed unless there are serious reasons for the changes. It is not unusual for people to tolerate bad treatment instead of starting a new government. However, sometimes a government goes too far. Sometimes the people have the right and the duty to overthrow the current government and form a new one.

The people of the colonies have suffered a long time under British rule. King George III has done many things to hurt the people of the colonies. To prove this is true, a list of facts about how the King has governed will be written for the world to see.

Facts About the Government of King George III and Parliament

The King has refused to agree to laws that are necessary for the public good.

He has forbidden the Governors of the colonies to pass important laws without his agreement. He has also failed to approve those laws.

He has refused to pass other laws that would affect large groups of people. The King refused to pass these laws unless the people gave up the right to have representation in the government. This representation is important to the people. The laws are only a threat to the King because he wants to have all of the power over the government.

He has forced the legislatures to meet in unusual and uncomfortable places far from the lawmakers' homes. These meetings have also been far from the places where the public records are kept. This has made it difficult for the legislators. The King has done this to tire the legislators and make them more willing to agree to his laws.

He has dissolved colonial legislatures. He has done this simply because they opposed his taking away the rights of the people.

After breaking up the legislatures, he has not allowed new legislatures to be elected. The power to make laws cannot be taken from the people. The people have that power. Without leadership, the colony is exposed to invasion from outsiders and rebellion from its people.

He has tried to stop the colonies from growing. He has done this by making it difficult for people from other countries to become citizens of the colonies. He has refused to pass laws that would encourage people to come and live in the colonies. He has made it difficult for people to establish themselves in new areas of the colonies.

He has made it difficult to provide justice to the people of the colonies. He has refused to allow laws that would give the courts the powers they need.

Judges must follow only the King's laws, or he removes them as judges. If a judge does not follow the King's wishes, that judge may lose his salary.

He has developed many new governmental offices and filled them with people who will do what he says. These people harass the colonists. These people's salaries are paid by the taxes the King places on the colonists.

He has kept standing armies in the colonies during peacetime. These armies have not been approved by the legislatures.

He has tried to make the army independent from the legislatures and the people. He has tried to make the army more powerful than the legislatures and the people.

He has worked with the English Parliament to make laws for the colonies. Together they have tried to force the colonies to follow these laws that do not agree with the colonial laws. These are laws that have not been agreed to by the people. A list of these laws follows.

They have quartered large groups of armed soldiers in the colonists' homes.

They have protected these soldiers, with mock trials, from punishment for crimes committed against the colonists. These crimes include murder.

They have cut off the colonies' trade with other countries of the world.

They have taxed the colonies without the agreement of the people.

They have taken away many people's right to a trial by jury.

They have taken colonists to England to be tried for crimes that were not committed.

They have abolished the free English law system in Quebec. In its place they have established bad laws and enlarged the province borders. This has been done to serve as an example to the colonists. It appears they may introduce the same absolute rule over the American colonies.

They have taken away many of the colonies' charters and most important laws. They have made changes that have a great effect on the governments of the colonies.

They have dissolved colonial legislatures. They have declared themselves the only power that can make laws for the colonies.

The King has given up his power over the colonial government. He has done this by declaring the colonies are not under the protection of England. He has gone to war against the colonies.

He has attacked our ships at sea, our coastal areas, burned our towns and ruined the lives of our people.

He is currently sending large armies of paid soldiers to finish the job of devastating and killing our people. He has done many cruel, barbaric and dishonest things. He is completely unworthy to be King and should not be allowed to rule a civilized country.

He has allowed colonists to be taken prisoner at sea. These prisoners have been forced to fight against other Americans.

He has promoted rebellions within the colonies. He has convinced the Indians to attack the colonies.

During the time King George has done all of these things, the colonists have humbly tried to get him to listen. The many petitions sent to the King have been answered with more injustice. King George has shown himself to be a tyrant. He is not fit to be the ruler of people who are free.

From time to time we have warned the British people about how the King and Parliament have treated us.

We have reminded the British of why we came to the colonies and settled here.

We have asked the British people to think about justice. We have asked them to remember the ties between our two peoples. We have asked them to think of what will result if the connection between us is broken. The British people have not responded in any way.

For these reasons, we must now separate from the British people. We will think of them as we think of the rest of the world's peoples. They will be our enemies in times of war. They will be our friends in times of peace.

Separation Statement

We, the representatives of the United States of America, are meeting in Congress. We appeal to God, in the name of the people, for approval of our actions. We declare these colonies to be free and independent states. The colonies no longer have any loyalty to the British King. All political ties between the colonies and Great Britain are totally dissolved. As free and independent states, they have the power to make war and peace. The states may make agreements with other countries, trade with other countries and do any other things that independent states have the right to do.

In complete support of this Declaration, and with a firm belief in God, we all pledge our lives, our fortunes and our honor to each other.

The Declaration of Independence

IN CONGRESS, July 4, 1776

A DECLARATION

By the REPRESENTATIVES of the UNITED STATES OF AMERICA, In GENERAL CONGRESS assembled

When in the Course of human Events, it becomes necessary for one People to dissolve the Political Bands which have connected them with another, and to assume among the Powers of the Earth, the separate and equal Station to which the Laws of Nature and of Nature's God entitle them, a decent Respect to the Opinions of Mankind requires that they should declare the causes which impel them to the Separation.

We hold these Truths to be self-evident, that all Men are created equal, that they are endowed by their Creator with certain unalienable Rights, that among these are Life, Liberty, and the Pursuit of Happiness—That to secure these Rights, Governments are instituted among Men, deriving their just Powers from the Consent of the Governed, that whenever any Form of Government becomes destructive of these Ends, it is the Right of the People to alter or to abolish it, and to institute new Government, laying its Foundation on such Principles, and organizing its Powers in such Form, as to them shall seem most likely to effect their Safety and Happiness. Prudence, indeed, will dictate that Governments long established should not be changed for light and transient Causes; and accordingly all Experience hath shewn, that Mankind are more disposed to suffer, while Evils are sufferable, than to right themselves by abolishing the Forms to which they are accustomed. But when a long Train of Abuses and Usurpations, pursuing invariably the same Object, evinces a Design to reduce them under absolute Despotism, it is their Right, it is their Duty, to throw off such

Government, and to provide new Guards for their future Security. Such has been the patient Sufferance of these Colonies; and such is now the Necessity which constrains them to alter their former Systems of Government. The History of the present King of Great-Britain is a History of repeated Injuries and Usurpations, all having in direct Object the Establishment of an absolute Tyranny over these States. To prove this, let Facts be submitted to a candid World.

He has refused his Assent to Laws, the most wholesome and necessary for the public Good.

He has forbidden his Governors to pass Laws of immediate and pressing Importance, unless suspended in their Operation till his Assent should be obtained; and when so suspended, he has utterly neglected to attend to them.

He has refused to pass other Laws for the Accommodation of large Districts of People, unless those People would relinquish the Right of Representation in the Legislature, a Right inestimable to them, and formidable to Tyrants only.

He has called together Legislative Bodies at Places unusual, uncomfortable, and distant from the Depository of their Public Records, for the sole Purpose of fatiguing them into Compliance with his Measures.

He has dissolved Representative Houses repeatedly, for opposing with manly Firmness his Invasions on the Rights of the People.

He has refused for a long Time, after such Dissolutions, to cause others to be elected; whereby the Legislative Powers, incapable of Annihilation, have returned to the People at large for their exercise; the State remaining in the mean time exposed to all the Dangers of Invasion from without, and Convulsions within.

He has endeavoured to prevent the Population of these States; for that Purpose obstructing the Laws for Naturalization of Foreigners; refusing to pass others to encourage their Migrations hither, and raising the Conditions of new Appropriations of Lands.

He has obstructed the Administration of Justice, by refusing his Assent to Laws for establishing Judiciary Powers.

He has made Judges dependent on his Will alone, for the Tenure of their Offices, and the Amount and payment of their Salaries.

He has erected a Multitude of new Offices, and sent hither Swarms of Officers to harrass our People, and eat out their Substance.

He has kept among us, in Times of Peace, Standing Armies, without the consent of our Legislatures.

He has affected to render the Military independent of, and superior to the Civil Power.

He has combined with others to subject us to a Jurisdiction foreign to our Constitution, and unacknowledged by our Laws; giving his Assent to their Acts of pretended Legislation:

For quartering large Bodies of Armed Troops among us:

For protecting them, by a mock Trial, from Punishment for any Murders which they should commit on the Inhabitants of these States:

For cutting off our Trade with all Parts of the World:

For imposing Taxes on us without our Consent:

For depriving us, in many Cases, of the Benefits of Trial by Jury:

For transporting us beyond Seas to be tried for pretended Offences:

For abolishing the free System of English Laws in a neighbouring Province, establishing therein an arbitrary Government, and enlarging its Boundaries, so as to render it at once an Example and fit Instrument for introducing the same absolute Rule into these Colonies:

For taking away our Charters, abolishing our most valuable Laws, and altering fundamentally the Forms of our Governments:

For suspending our own Legislatures, and declaring themselves invested with Power to legislate for us in all Cases whatsoever.

He has abdicated Government here, by declaring us out of his Protection and waging War against us.

He has plundered our Seas, ravaged our Coasts, burnt our towns, and destroyed the Lives of our People.

He is, at this Time, transporting large Armies of foreign Mercenaries to complete the works of Death, Desolation, and Tyranny, already begun with circumstances of Cruelty and Perfidy, scarcely paralleled in the most barbarous Ages, and totally unworthy the Head of a civilized Nation.

He has constrained our fellow Citizens taken Captive on the high Seas to bear Arms against their Country, to become the Executioners of their Friends and Brethren, or to fall themselves by their Hands.

He has excited domestic Insurrections amongst us, and has endeavoured to bring on the Inhabitants of our Frontiers, the merciless Indian Savages, whose known Rule of Warfare, is an undistinguished Destruction, of all Ages, Sexes and Conditions.

In every stage of these Oppressions we have Petitioned for Redress in the most humble Terms: Our repeated Petitions have been answered only by repeated Injury.

A Prince, whose Character is thus marked by every act which may define a Tyrant, is unfit to be the Ruler of a free People.

Nor have we been wanting in Attentions to our British Brethren. We have warned them from Time to Time of Attempts by their Legislature to extend an unwarrantable Jurisdiction over us. We have reminded them of the Circumstances of our Emigration and Settlement here. We have appealed to their native Justice and Magnanimity, and we have conjured them by the Ties of our common Kindred to disavow these Usurpations, which, would inevitably interrupt our Connections and Correspondence. They too have been deaf to the Voice of Justice and of Consanguinity. We must, therefore, acquiesce in the Necessity, which denounces our Separation, and hold them, as we hold the rest of Mankind, Enemies in War, in Peace, Friends.

We, therefore, the Representatives of the UNITED STATES OF AMERICA, in General Congress, Assembled, appealing to the Supreme Judge of the World for the Rectitude of our Intentions, do, in the Name, and by Authority of the good People of these Colonies, solemnly Publish and Declare, That these United Colonies are, and of Right ought to be, Free and Independent States; that they are absolved from all Allegiance to the British Crown, and that all political Connection between them and the State of Great-Britain, is and ought to be totally dissolved; and that as Free and Independent States, they have full Power to levy War, conclude Peace, contract Alliances, establish Commerce, and to do all other Acts and Things which Independent States may of right do. And for the support of this declaration, with a firm Reliance on the Protection of divine Providence, we mutually pledge to each other our lives, our Fortunes, and our sacred Honor.

Historical Notes

The First Continental Congress was held in Philadelphia, Pennsylvania in 1774. This was the first opportunity for the colonies to meet and discuss the possibility of forming a new government. The Second Continental Congress was composed of representatives of all thirteen colonies. During the Revolutionary War this group wrote a new plan for the government called the Articles of Confederation. After living under the rule of King George, the writers of this plan made sure the federal government did not have too much power. Unfortunately, this resulted in the federal government lacking the power to collect taxes, coin money or enforce laws. There was no chief executive or judicial branch, only a legislative branch in which each state had one vote. The weaknesses in the Articles of Confederation resulted in a convention being held in Philadelphia in 1787 to rewrite this plan. Once it was decided that the Articles could not reasonably be rewritten, the delegates began writing an entirely new plan, the U.S. Constitution.

During the Constitutional Convention many ideas were presented. Each state had different ideas and there was much disagreement. Many people believe that without the strong leadership of George Washington the U.S. Constitution might never have been completed. The delegates generally agreed that the federal government should be composed of a legislative, judicial and executive branch. This design allowed for a system of checks and balances. This would keep any one branch from gaining too much power and it requires the governmental branches to work together. They also agreed that the people of the nation might not make good choices in selecting a President. The result is the Electoral College, in which the people vote for electors and the electors vote to elect the President.

Even after the general form of the Constitution was decided, there were two critical areas that continued to be sources of great disagreement. The first dealt with providing fair representation for all states. The Virginia Plan gave each state a certain number of representatives to Congress based on that state's population. The smaller states did not think this was such a great idea. The New Jersey Plan suggested that each state have one vote in Congress, regardless of population. The larger states were not happy with this idea. Fortunately, the Great Compromise was able to combine these two plans. The result is a bicameral (two house) legislature. The upper house of Congress, the Senate, is made up of two representatives from each state. Membership in the lower house, the House of Representatives, is based on state population.

The second major problem was dealing with the issue of slavery. Many Northerners wanted to abolish it entirely. In addition, they did not want slaves counted for representation purposes.. The Southerners did not want to abolish slavery but they did want slaves counted as part of the state population. A compromise finally resulted in each slave being counted as three-fifths of a person (for the purpose of determining how many Representatives a state could have in the House), and it was decided that the slave trade would be allowed to continue until at least 1808.

The first state to ratify the Constitution of the United States was Delaware, on December 7, 1787. When the Constitution was ratified by the ninth state (New Hampshire) on June 21, 1788, the required two-thirds of the states had signed and the document went into effect. New York and Virginia refused to sign until they were assured that a bill of rights would soon be added. In all, it took over two years for all thirteen states to ratify the U.S. Constitution.

Constitution of the United States

Preamble

The Preamble to the Constitution is the introduction. It says the people are writing the Constitution in an effort to:

- make the country better by establishing a system of justice,
- insure peace within the country,
- provide for the nation's defense,
- promote the general welfare of the people, and
- provide freedom for the citizens of the nation and their children.

The Preamble states that the authority for the Constitution comes from the people.

Article I

Article I talks about the legislative, or lawmaking, branch of the government.

Section 1 — Congress

Congress has all lawmaking powers for the country. Congress is composed of two houses: the Senate and the House of Representatives.

Section 2 — The House of Representatives

Members of the House of Representatives are elected by the people in the state they will represent. They are elected to two year terms. Residents of each state who are eligible to vote for state legislators may vote for Representatives to the House.

A Representative must be at least twenty-five years old. That person must also be a U.S. citizen for at least seven years, and a resident of the state he or she represents.

A national count, or census, of the people is taken every ten years. When the Constitution was written, slaves were counted as three-fifths of a person. Indians who were not taxed were not counted at all. The census is conducted in years ending with zero. State population numbers from the census are important. These numbers are used to decide the number of Representatives each state is allowed. No state may have more than one Representative per thirty thousand residents. Every state must have at least one Representative in the House. (Later, Congress decided that 435 members would be the maximum number of Representatives in the House.)

If a vacancy occurs in the House, Representatives cannot be chosen by governmental officials. Representatives must be elected by the people of the state they represent.

The leader of the House of Representatives is elected by the Representatives. The leader is called the Speaker. The only governmental body that may impeach government officials is the House. Impeach means to decide to put a public official on trial for wrongdoing or misconduct. The actual impeachment trial is held in the Senate.

Section 3 — The Senate

Each state elects two Senators regardless of how big or small the state's population.

Senators are elected to six year terms. (The Constitution said Senators were chosen by state legislatures but this was changed by the Seventeenth Amendment. Now the people of each state elect their Senators.) Each Senator has one vote.

Only one third of the Senate is elected every two years. Because of this, the Senate changes more slowly than the House of Representatives. If a Senator dies, resigns or otherwise vacates the office, the Governor of that state appoints a replacement. This person serves in the Senate until an election can be held. Then the people of the state vote to elect a new Senator. (Prior to the Seventeenth Amendment, the Governor appointed someone until an election could be held in the state legislature.)

A Senator must be at least thirty years old and a citizen of the U.S. for at least nine years. That person must also be a resident of the state that he or she represents.

The leader of the Senate is called the President of the Senate. This office is held by the Vice-President of the United States. The President of the Senate may vote only if a tie needs to be broken.

If the President of the Senate is absent, the President *pro tempore* is the leader. The President *pro tempore* is a temporary president. This person, and all other Senate officers, are elected by the members of the Senate.

Impeachment trials may only be held in the Senate. When judging an official in an impeachment trial, the Senators are under oath. If the U.S. President is on trial, the Chief Justice of the Supreme Court acts as the judge. A minimum two-thirds vote by the Senators is needed to find an official guilty in an impeachment trial.

If the Senate finds an official guilty, that person may be removed from office. He or she may also be kept from holding a future public office. These are the two harshest penalties allowed. However, the official may also be tried in the regular courts if a law has been broken. Other punishments may be given, if he or she is found guilty there.

Section 4 — Congressional Elections and Meetings

Each state legislature decides when elections for the U.S. Congress will take place. Congress has the power to make or change laws about elections. However, Congress may not make laws about the places chosen by the state legislatures for the election of Senators.

The U.S. Congress must meet at least one time each year. Originally the date was the first Monday in December but this was later changed by the Twentieth Amendment. The date is now January 3.

Section 5 — Responsibilities of the Congress

Each house of Congress decides its own rules. Each house has the power to say if its members are qualified and fairly elected. If there is a question about who has won an election to the Senate or the House of Representatives, that house of Congress decides the winner. A majority of the members must be present to have a quorum. A quorum is needed to conduct business. Each house makes its own rules about requiring its members to attend meetings.

The House of Representatives and the Senate each make their own rules. Each house has the authority to punish its own members for disorderly behavior. To expel a member, a two-thirds vote of that house is necessary.

Each house must keep a published, public journal of what is said in its meetings. This journal is called the Congressional Record. The only time information discussed in congressional meetings is not published is when the meetings must be held in secret to protect the safety of the country. If one-fifth of the members of either house request it, a record of how each member voted on a bill is included in the journal.

While Congress is in session, the House and Senate must meet frequently. Unless both houses agree to a break, no more than three days may pass without a meeting. In addition, neither house may have meetings separately in locations away from the other house.

Section 6 — Rights and Responsibilities of Members of Congress

Salaries for members of Congress are paid out of the U.S. Treasury. The amount to be paid is decided by law. Except for cases of treason, felony or breach of the peace, members of the House and Senate cannot be arrested while attending, going to or leaving congressional meetings. The members cannot be punished for anything they say during their meetings.

During their terms in office, members of Congress may not have any other jobs in the U.S. government.

Section 7 — How a Bill Becomes a Law

All bills for raising money (tax bills) must come from the House of Representatives. The Senate may suggest or agree with amendments to these bills.

To become a law, a bill must first pass votes in the House and Senate. After passing these votes, the bill is sent to the President for his or her signature. If the President agrees with the bill and signs it within ten days, the bill becomes a law. If the President disagrees with the bill, he or she may veto it. If the bill is vetoed, it is returned to the house where it originated. The President must also send his or her reasons for objecting to the bill.

The house discusses the bill again and a vote is taken. If more than two-thirds of the members agree to pass the bill, it is sent to the other house. The President's arguments against the bill are also sent to the other house. The other house discusses the bill and takes a vote. If two-thirds of that house agrees, the bill passes and becomes a law, in spite of the President's objections. For this vote, each house must record which members voted for and against the bill.

If a bill is not returned by the President within ten days (excepting Sundays), it is treated just the same as it would be if the President had signed it. The bill becomes a law. The only time this is not the case, is if the Congress is not in session so the President cannot return the bill. If this happens, the bill does not become a law.

All matters that require both houses to agree must be presented to the President. The two-thirds vote required to overrule the President's veto applies to these matters. The only exception to this rule is a vote to adjourn meetings.

Section 8 — Powers of the Congress

Congress has the following powers:

- to collect taxes;
- to spend money to pay the nation's debts and provide for the people's protection and welfare (but all taxes have to be the same across the country);
- to borrow money;
- to make rules about trade between the states, between the U.S. and the Indian tribes, and between the U.S. and foreign countries;
- to make rules for people from other countries to become American citizens;
- to make rules that apply in all states about people who cannot pay their bills;
- to make money and decide how much it is worth;
- to determine a set of weights and measures;
- to make laws for punishing people who counterfeit U.S. government bonds, stamps or money;

- to set up a postal system and roads;

- to give patents to inventors and copyrights to authors to help the progress of the arts and sciences; and

- to set up a system of courts with less power than the Supreme Court.

Congress also has these powers:

- to determine laws and punishments for crimes against American ships and against international law;

- to declare war and to give soldiers the power to fight enemies and take their property;

- to form an army and pay its soldiers, but not for more than two years at a time;

- to form and maintain a navy;

- to make rules for the operation of the army and navy;

- to use the states' militia (National Guard) if necessary to enforce the nation's laws, to keep rebellions from occurring, or to keep foreign countries from invading the U.S.;

- to form and maintain the militia, to make rules for the operation and training of the militia (but the states choose the militia officers);

- to make all laws for the District of Columbia and for all property bought by the U.S. (like forts, shipyards, and other governmental buildings); and

- to make any laws necessary to carry out the powers granted in the Constitution.

Section 9 — Powers Not Given to the Congress

Congress may not restrict the importation of slaves before 1808. However, a tax of up to ten dollars may be charged for each slave.

Anyone charged with committing a crime must be taken to court and told why they are being held. This is called a writ of habeus corpus. The judge then decides if this is a valid reason to hold the person. This right is guaranteed to all Americans. However, it may not take place if a rebellion or invasion is taking place and it is more important to protect the public safety.

No bill of attainder laws are allowed. This means that a trial in court is required before a person may be punished for a crime. In addition, no one may be tried under ex post facto laws. These laws would allow people to be punished for doing something that was not a crime when they committed the action.

No one can be taxed at a flat rate unless everyone is taxed the same amount. (This was later changed by the Sixteenth Amendment.)

Goods leaving any state cannot be taxed by Congress. Trade laws must be fair and equal for all of the states. Ships cannot be taxed for going from one state to another.

Unless both houses pass a bill, and the President signs it, no U.S. government money may be spent. Congress has to let the people know how much money has been taken in and how much has been spent.

No one may be given a title of nobility, such as knight, duchess, or baron. Government workers may not accept gifts, money, jobs or titles from any other country. The only exception to this rule is if Congress agrees.

Section 10 — Limitations on the States

No state can make a treaty or agreement with another country. No state may give its people the right to work against another country. No state may make its own money.

States are not allowed to use anything but gold and silver for money. No state may sentence a person to death without a trial by jury and witnesses. No state may punish a person for something he or she did before it became a crime. Private agreements and contracts may not be changed by the passage of state laws. States may not grant titles of nobility.

No state may tax goods coming into or going out of state. The exception to this rule is if Congress agrees to a tax for the purpose of paying for state inspection laws. If a tax is allowed, the money collected is sent to the national government. Congress may change laws about these state taxes.

No state may put a tax on ships. No state can have its own army, except the state militia, or keep warships during times of peace. No state can make agreements with other states or other countries without permission from Congress. Unless it is attacked and cannot avoid fighting, no state may go to war.

Article II

Article III talks about the executive, or law enforcing, department of the government.

Section 1 — The President and the Vice President

The President is the chief executive of the United States. The term of office for the President is four years. The term of office for the Vice President is also four years.

What follows is how the Constitution says the President and Vice President are elected. (However, the Twelfth Amendment changed much of how this is done.)

First, each state selects people called electors who vote for presidential candidates. These people make up a group called the Electoral College. Each state has a number of electors equal to the number of Representatives and Senators from that state. No one who holds an office in the government may be an elector. This includes Senators and Representatives.

The electors meet in their own state and vote by ballot for two of the presidential candidates. [The Twelfth Amendment changes this to one presidential candidate and one vice presidential candidate.] At least one of the candidates must be from another state.

A list is made of all the candidates and how many votes each received. The electors sign the list and it is sealed. [The Twelfth Amendment requires two lists, one for President and one for Vice President. The rest of the procedures stay the same, except that two lists are used.]

The list is then sent to the President of the Senate in Washington, D.C. The President of the Senate opens the list in front of the Senate and House of Representatives. The votes are counted and the person with the most votes becomes the next President of the United States. This person must receive votes from more than half of the electors.

If there is a tie, and more than one candidate has over half of the votes, the House of Representatives votes. One of the candidates in the tie wins the vote and becomes the President. If no candidate has more than half of the elector votes, a vote is taken in the House. Members of the House vote for one of the top five candidates receiving the most votes. [The Twelfth Amendment changes this to the top three candidates.] However, each state has only one vote. At least two-thirds of the states must be represented and the winner must receive over half of the votes.

The candidate with the second highest number of votes becomes the Vice President. If there is a tie at this point, the Senate elects the Vice President. [This has changed.

The Twelfth Amendment requires a separate list for the Vice Presidential candidates. The President of the Senate follows the same procedures as with the Presidential list. Another change is that electors now follow the choices of candidates made by the political parties at their national conventions. These conventions take place sometime before November in the year of the election. Candidates for President and Vice President are chosen at these conventions. The people of the United States vote in November. On the ballot are the names of the candidates and/or the electors and the names of the candidates they support. The electors vote in December and the votes are counted in front of Congress.]

Congress decides when electors are selected by the states. [In 1872, Congress decided that day should take place every fourth year on the Tuesday after the first Monday in November.]

The President of the United States must be a natural born citizen. This person must also be at least thirty-five years old and have been a resident of the United States for at least fourteen years.

If the President resigns, dies, or for some other reason cannot do the job, the Vice President takes over. If both the President and Vice President are unable to do the job, Congress appoints someone to do it. This person does the job until either the President or Vice President can again do the work, or until a new person is elected. [All of this changed over time. In 1886, Congress made a law that places the Secretary of State (followed by other Cabinet members) next in the line of succession. In 1947, Congress changed the law again. Now, the Speaker of the House and then the President *pro tempore* of the Senate come before the Secretary of State. The other members of the Cabinet follow the Secretary of State. Congress changed things again in 1967, with the Twenty-Fifth Amendment. This amendment says that if the Vice President becomes President, that person may choose his or her new Vice President. Both houses of Congress must approve of the person he or she chooses.]

The President must be paid. The salary may not be increased or decreased while the President is in office. This is the only pay the President may receive from the country or any of the states.

The President must take the oath of office before beginning the job. [This oath is usually taken on January 20. The Chief Justice of the Supreme Court usually conducts the swearing in ceremony.] This oath says that he or she will be faithful in his or her work as President. The oath also says that the President will protect and defend the Constitution.

Section 2 — Powers of the President

The President is the Commander-in-Chief of the army and navy. He or she is also the commander of the National Guard when there is a national need for their services.

The Cabinet is made up of the people in charge of the executive departments of the government (like the Secretary of Defense or the Secretary of State). These people are selected by the President and serve as presidential advisors. The President may ask any member of the Cabinet questions relating to that person's department.

The President can grant reprieves and pardons. He or she can do this for anyone who has committed a crime against the government, except a person who has been impeached.

The President can make treaties with other countries. However, he or she can only do this if two-thirds of the Senators present agree. The President chooses ambassadors to represent the U.S. in other countries. He or she also appoints Supreme Court justices, and other federal officials. However, the Senate must approve these choices. Congress may make laws so that decisions on less important jobs can be made by the President, the courts or the members of the Cabinet.

The President may choose people to fill positions if the Senate is not in session. These positions expire at the end of the next session of the Senate.

Section 3 — Responsibilities of the President

From time to time, the President must make a speech to Congress about how the country is doing. This is called the State of the Union address. In this speech, the President also makes suggestions on how things could be improved. If it is important, the President may call either house or both houses of Congress together for a special meeting. If the two houses cannot agree on when to end the meeting, the President can decide when to adjourn.

It is the President's job to meet with the representatives of other countries. The President must make sure that the laws of the United States are obeyed. The President also chooses government officers.

Section 4 — Impeachment

In cases of treason, bribery, or other wrongdoing, the President, Vice President and all other government officers may be impeached by the House. They may be tried before the Senate. If they are found guilty of the charges, they may be removed from office.

Article III

Article III talks about the judicial, or judging, branch of the government.

Section 1 — United States Courts

The highest court in the United States is the Supreme Court. Congress has the power to establish other, lower courts. The Supreme Court hears cases between states. Cases that have come up from the U.S. District Courts and then the Circuit Courts of

Appeals may also be heard by the Supreme Court. A judgment made by the Supreme Court is the law of the land. Supreme Court justices and the judges of the lower federal courts are selected by the President and approved by the Senate.

As long as they are not impeached and do not commit crimes, U.S. court judges and justices keep their jobs for life or until they choose to resign. Pay for justices and lower court judges cannot be reduced during their term of service.

Section 2 — Types of Cases Heard in the Federal Courts

The Supreme Court has the power to decide if laws are in keeping with the U.S. Constitution. [This is called the power of judicial review.] If a law is found to be unconstitutional, it can be thrown out.

The federal court system deals with cases that involve:

- the Constitution,
- the laws of the United States,
- government treaties,
- government officials,
- laws that apply to ships,
- the breaking of federal laws,
- disagreements between states,
- disagreements between a state and a resident of a different state [this was removed by the Eleventh Amendment, so that these cases cannot be heard in federal courts],

- two or more people who live in different states,
- people who claim land in another state,
- a state or a citizen of the United States and foreign countries or citizens.

In cases that involve a state or a representative of a foreign country, the Supreme Court has original jurisdiction. This means the Supreme Court is the first court to hear the case and render a decision. All the other types of cases heard by the Supreme Court are heard first in the lower courts. In these cases, the Supreme Court has appellate jurisdiction. This means the Supreme Court is a court of appeals, after the case has first been heard in a lower court. After a verdict has been rendered in the lower court, the case may be appealed to the Supreme Court. Congress may make laws about what types of cases may be appealed. All decisions made by the Supreme Court are final. [However, Congress can pass amendments to the Constitution that disagree with Supreme Court decisions. The Supreme Court must abide by all Constitutional amendments that are ratified.]

Except for impeachment trials, anyone accused of a crime has the right to a trial by jury. The trial must be held in the state where the crime was committed. If the crime did not take place in a state, Congress decides where the trial will be held.

Section 3 — Treason

Treason means going against one's own country. This can happen if a person goes to war against the country or helps the country's enemies.

To convict a person of treason, two witnesses who saw the person commit the act must testify. The only other way to convict a person of treason, is if the person confesses to the act in court.

Congress decides the punishment for a person convicted of treason. This punishment must end when the convicted person dies. The family of the convicted person cannot be punished.

Article IV

Section 1 — The States

Every state must respect the laws, records and court decisions of all other states. Congress may make laws to say how this will be done.

Section 2 — Citizen Rights

The citizens of each state will have the same rights in any other state.

A person charged with a felony, treason or another crime who leaves the state may face extradition. This means that the Governor of the state where the crime was committed may ask the Governor of the state where the person was caught to send that person back to the first state to face trial.

Slaves do not become free simply by leaving slave states. They shall be returned to their owners. [Now that there are no slaves in the U.S. this paragraph has little meaning. However, when the Constitution was being written this was important. The slave states refused to sign the Constitution unless this paragraph was included.]

Section 3 — New States

States may become part of the United States with approval from Congress. States usually begin as U.S. territories. They become states after Congress and the President approve the state's constitution. No new state may be made from a part of an established state. However, during the Civil War, Congress and President

Lincoln split Virginia into two states: Virginia and West Virginia. West Virginians were Union supporters, while Virginia was part of the Confederacy.

Congress makes rules and regulations about all federal lands.

Section 4 — State's Rights

Every state must have a republican form of government, one in which the people elect the leaders. The federal government shall protect the states from being invaded by other countries. The President can send soldiers if necessary to keep the peace in a state.

Article V

Amending the Constitution

A constitutional amendment may be proposed if two-thirds of both houses of Congress agree. An amendment may also be proposed if two-thirds of the state legislatures ask for a Constitutional Convention.

For an amendment to be added to the Constitution, it must be ratified by the legislatures of three-fourths of the states. Another way for this to happen is if three-fourths of the states have conventions and approve the amendment. Congress decides which of these two ways will be used.

Prior to 1808, no amendment could be written changing the part of Article I dealing with returning slaves to their owners. No amendment may change the part of Article I that talks about directly taxing the people. No amendment may change the two Senators per state provision in Article I.

Article VI

Payment of the Nation's Debt

All debts owed by the nation before the Constitution was adopted are still valid and will be paid.

The laws of the country, the Constitution, and treaties made by the United States are the supreme law of the land. (Federal law is higher than state laws. If two laws are in conflict, the federal law is followed.)

All members of Congress, all state government officers, and all judges must swear to follow the Constitution. They must follow the Constitution even if it disagrees with state laws.

No religious test will ever be made a requirement of holding a government office.

Article VII

The Ratification and Signing of the Constitution

The Constitution shall go into effect after being signed by nine states (that was two-thirds of the original thirteen states).

On September 17, 1787, thirty-nine state delegates from twelve states signed the Constitution and it was ratified. (Rhode Island had not sent any delegates to attend the meeting.)

Bill of Rights — Study Guide

(The first ten amendments make up the Bill of Rights)

Amendment 1

(The People's Right to be Free)

Congress may not make any laws restricting freedom of religion. People may worship in any way that they wish.

Congress may not make laws that restrict freedom of speech. People may say or print what they wish.

Congress may not make laws restricting the people's right to assemble and meet peacefully. The people may also petition the government about things they believe need to be changed.

Amendment 2

(The People's Right to Protect Themselves)

Each state has the right to keep a state militia. The people have the right to keep and bear arms (guns).

Amendment 3

(The People's Right not to be Forced to House Soldiers)

Soldiers may not be quartered in civilian's homes without the homeowner's permission. In times of war, soldiers may stay in people's homes but only in agreement with the law.

Amendment 4

(The People's Right to Privacy and Protection from Search and Seizure)

No one's person (self), house, papers or other possessions may be searched without a search warrant. Unreasonable searches and seizures are forbidden. A search warrant may be granted by the court only if the person asking for the warrant swears that there is a good reason for the search. The search warrant must say where the search will take place, who the people are, and what will be searched. The search warrant must also say what the searchers expect to find.

Amendment 5

(The People's Right to a Fair Trial in Open Court)

No one may be tried for a serious crime unless a grand jury says there is enough evidence to warrant a trial. A serious crime is one that could result in the death penalty or in a jail or prison sentence. A grand jury is composed of twelve to twenty-three people who hear witnesses in secret. After a grand jury indictment, the accused person is tried in public before another jury. When the country is in danger, cases involving the army, navy, or militia do not require a grand jury. No one may be tried a second time for a crime for which they have been found not guilty. No one can be forced to incriminate themselves in a criminal trial. No one can have their life, freedom or property taken without due process of law. Private property may not be taken by the government unless the owner has been paid a fair price.

Amendment 6

(The People's Rights in Court)

Anyone accused of a crime is guaranteed a speedy and public trial. The jury must be impartial. Jury members must reside in the state and district where the crime took place. The accused person must be told why he or she is on trial. Witnesses must give their testimony in front of the person accused of the crime. The judge has the power to force witnesses to give their testimony in court. If a person is accused of a crime, that person has the right to have an attorney represent them in court.

Amendment 7

(The People's Right to Jury Trials)

In any court case involving more than twenty dollars, the people in the case may ask for a jury trial. Once a jury makes a decision, that decision cannot be changed except by the courts as provided by law.

Amendment 8

(The People's Right to Fair Punishment)

Excessive bail is not allowed. Bail is money paid by the accused person as a promise that the person will come to his or her trial. If the person flees, he or she forfeits the bail money. Excessive fines are not allowed. Prisoners cannot be forced to endure cruel and unusual punishments.

Amendment 9

(Other Rights of the People)

Although the Constitution lists many rights, the people have many other rights that are not listed.

Amendment 10

(Rights of the States and the People)

The people and the states have all the powers that have not been given to the U.S. government by the Constitution. All powers not prohibited by the Constitution belong to the states and the people as well.

Amendment 11

(Cases Against States, *Ratified 1795*)

The U.S. courts will not hear cases brought against any state by a citizen of another state or country. (This changed the Constitution, Article III, Section 2.)

Amendment 12

(Electing the President and Vice President, *Ratified 1804*)

The electors meet in their states and vote for a President and Vice President. At least one of these people must be from a different state. The electors vote for candidates for each office. After the voting, a list is made for the office of President. Another list is written for the office of Vice President. The candidates for each office and the number of votes each received are listed. The electors sign their names, seal the lists, and send them to the President of the Senate.

In a meeting with both houses of Congress, the President of the Senate opens the lists and the votes are counted. The person with the most votes, and more than half the votes, for the office of President becomes the President. If no one has over half of the votes, the House members vote on no more than the top three candidates. The person with the most votes becomes the President. Each state has only one vote. At least two-thirds of the states must vote for the election to be valid. The candidate who wins must have votes from more than half of the states. If the House does not elect a President by March 4, the Vice President becomes the Acting President. (The Twentieth Amendment changed this date to January 20.)

From the second list, the person with the most electoral votes, and more than half of them, becomes the Vice President. If no candidate has more than half of the votes, the Senate votes on the top two candidates. For the vote to be valid, two-thirds of the Senators must vote. Votes from more than half of all the Senators (fifty-one or more) are required for a candidate to win. If the Constitution keeps a person from becoming President, that person may not run for the office of Vice President either.

Amendment 13

(Abolition of Slavery, *Ratified 1865*)

In the United States, no one may be made a slave. No one may be forced to work for someone else, except in cases where the courts are punishing someone for a crime. Congress has the power to make laws to enforce this amendment.

Amendment 14

(Citizenship, Representation, Broken Oaths, Civil War Debts, *Ratified 1868*)

Section 1: Citizenship

Anyone born in this country or made a citizen is a citizen of the United States. U.S. citizens are under the rule of the U.S. government. In addition, any citizen of the U.S. is also a citizen of the state where he or she lives. States cannot make or follow laws that take away the rights of U.S. citizens. Unless due process of law is followed, no state may take a person's life, freedom or property. All states must provide citizens equal protection under the law.

Section 2: Representation

The number of Representatives a state will have in the House depends on that state's population. For this purpose, all people within each state are counted except for untaxed Indians. No state may keep eligible male voters from voting in any state or federal election. If a state does this, that state will lose Representatives in the House according to the number kept from voting. "Eligible voter" means a male citizen, over 21 years of age, who has not committed any crimes that would keep him from voting.

Section 3: Broken Oaths

No one may hold a government office if he or she took the oath of office and then rebelled against the U.S. However, with a two-thirds vote of both houses, Congress may allow such a person to hold a government office.

Section 4: Civil War Debts

The U.S. government will pay lawful debts that result from fighting against rebellion. The payment of these debts will not be questioned. The U.S. will pay Union soldiers for their work in fighting the rebellion. The U.S. will also pay these soldier's pensions. The U.S. will not pay any debts the Confederacy has from fighting the Union. The states may not pay the Confederate debts either.

Section 5

Congress has the power to make laws to enforce this amendment.

Amendment 15

(The Right to Vote, *Ratified 1870*)

Section 1

A U.S. citizen's right to vote cannot be taken away as the result of that person's race or color. The right to vote cannot be taken away simply because a person was once a slave.

Section 2

Congress has the power to make laws to enforce this amendment.

Amendment 16

(Income Tax, *Ratified 1913*)

Congress has the power to collect taxes on people's income. Congress does not have to take any certain amount from each state.

Amendment 17

(The Election of Senators, *Ratified 1913*)

The people of each state elect two Senators. (This changes the Constitution, Article I, Section 3.) Senators have one vote each and serve six year terms. Anyone who can vote for members of the state legislature may also vote for Senators.

If a vacancy occurs in the Senate, the Governor of that state calls for an election to be held to fill the position. If the state legislature chooses to do so, it may allow the Governor to appoint a replacement. This temporary Senator serves until an election can be held. The legislature determines when and how the election will be held.

This amendment does not change the election of any Senator chosen before it took effect. It does not change the term of office for any Senator chosen prior to its adoption either.

Amendment 18

(Prohibition, *Ratified 1919*)

Section 1

This amendment will go into effect one year after three-fourths of the states ratify it. This amendment says that it is against the law to make, sell or transport intoxicating liquors. These liquors may not be brought into or sent out of the United States.

Section 2

Congress and the states have the power to make laws to enforce this amendment.

Section 3

The state legislatures have a time limit of seven years to approve this amendment. If they do not, the amendment will not become part of the Constitution.

Amendment 19

(Women's Right to Vote, *Ratified 1920*)

Section 1

No state may keep a citizen from voting simply because she is a woman.

Section 2

Congress has the power to make laws necessary to enforce this amendment.

Amendment 20

(Changes in Term Dates and Temporary President, *Ratified 1933*)

Section 1: New Dates for Terms of Office

The terms of office for President and Vice President will end at noon on January 20. The terms of Senators and Representatives will end at noon on January 3. New officers begin their terms when the preceding officer's terms end. (This changes the Constitution, Articles I and II as well as the Twelfth Amendment.)

Section 2: When Congress Meets

Congress will meet at least once a year. That meeting will take place at noon on January 3, unless a different day is determined by law. (This changes the Constitution, Article I, Section 4.)

Section 3: Temporary President

If the President-elect dies before taking office, the person elected Vice President serves as President. If no President has been elected when the term of office begins, the Vice President-elect becomes the Acting President. The Acting President steps down when a new President is elected. If there is no elected President or Vice President, Congress can make a law saying who will be the Acting President. Congress may make laws about how the Acting President will be chosen. This person will serve until a President or Vice President has been elected.

Section 4

Congress can make laws about what will happen if the House must elect a President and then that person dies. Congress can also make laws about what will happen if the Senate elects a Vice President and then he or she dies.

Section 5

Sections 1 and 2 of this amendment take effect on October 15 after the states ratify the amendment.

Section 6

This amendment will not take effect unless it is approved by three-fourths of the states within seven years.

Amendment 21

(Repeal of Amendment 18, *Ratified 1933*)

Section 1

The Eighteenth Amendment to the Constitution is no longer law.

Section 2

Although alcohol is now legal, state liquor laws will be enforced.

Section 3

If the state legislatures do not approve this amendment within seven years, it will not become law.

Amendment 22

(Presidential Term Limit, *Ratified 1951*)

Section 1

No one may be elected President more than two times. No one who has been President, or Acting President for more than two years of someone else's term may be elected President more than one time. (In other words, no one may serve as President for more than ten years.) The President, at the time of this amendment's adoption, is exempt from this law.

Section 2

Three-fourths of the state legislatures must approve this amendment within seven years or it will not become law.

Amendment 23

(Presidential Voting Rights for Residents of Washington, D.C., *Ratified 1961*)

Section 1

The people of Washington, D.C. can choose electors. These electors will vote for candidates for President and Vice President. The number of electors will be the same as the number of representatives in Congress would be if the District was a state. However, the District cannot have more electors than the state with the smallest population. District electors will vote in presidential elections in the same way as electors from states. District electors will meet in the District and they will follow the Twelfth Amendment.

Section 2

Congress has the power to make laws necessary to enforce this amendment.

Amendment 24

(Taxes and Voting, *Ratified 1964*)

Section 1

No one may be kept from voting in federal elections simply because he or she did not pay state poll taxes or other taxes.

Section 2

Congress has the power to make laws necessary to enforce this amendment.

Amendment 25

(Presidential Succession, *Ratified 1967*)

Section 1

The Vice President will become President if the President resigns, dies or is removed from office.

Section 2

If there is no Vice President, the President nominates someone for the job. This person becomes Vice President if more than half of both houses approve.

Section 3

The President can write a letter saying he or she is no longer able to do the work of being President. This letter is given to the President *pro tempore* of the Senate and the Speaker of the House. If this happens, the Vice President becomes the Acting President. If the President later decides he or she can do the work, another letter is required.

Section 4

The executive officers can write a letter if they think the President is unable to do the work. These officers must include the Vice President and more than half of the Cabinet members. The letter is sent to both the Speaker of the House and the President *pro tempore* of the Senate. If this happens, the Vice President immediately becomes the Acting President.

The President can write a letter to the President *pro tempore* and the Speaker of the House saying he or she is able to do the work. When the President does this, he or she again takes control as President. However, if the Vice President and more than half of the Cabinet (or any other group determined by Congress) do not agree, they write a letter saying so. The Speaker of the House and the President *pro tempore* must receive this letter within four days. If this happens, Congress has twenty-one days in which to decide if the President is able to do the work. If Congress is not in session, the members have forty-eight hours in which to meet. Congress has twenty-one days after this meeting to make a decision. If two-thirds of each house votes that the President is unable to do the work, the Vice President continues as Acting President. If two-thirds of both houses vote that the President is able to do the work, the President resumes his or her work.

Amendment 26

(18-Year-Olds Right to Vote, *Ratified 1971*)

Section 1

Any citizen who will be eighteen years old by election day will be allowed to register and vote. This voting right applies to all local, state and federal elections.

Section 2

Congress has the power to pass laws to enforce this amendment.

Amendment 27

(Congressional Pay Raises, *Ratified 1992*)

No law that changes the amount of pay for U.S. Senators and Representatives may take effect until after an election for Representatives has taken place.

Constitution of the United States

1787

Article 1
Legislative Branch
House of Representatives
Senate

Article 2
Executive Branch

Article 3
Judicial Branch

Article 4
How states work together
Citizen's Rights
States's Rights

Article 5
Amending the Constitution

Article 6
Public debt
Supreme law of the land

Article 7
Ratification of the Constitution

The Bill of Rights

1791

Amendment 1

Freedom of religion
Freedom of speech
Freedom of the press
Freedom to peacefully assebble
Petition for redress of grievances

Amendment 2

Regulated militia
Right to bear arms

Amendment 3

Quartering soldiers

Amendment 4

Unreasonable search and seizure

Amendment 5

Grand jury indictments for capital crimes
Double jeopardy
Self incrimination
Due process of law
Eminent domain

Amendment 6

Fair and speed trial

Amendment 7

Trial by jury

Amendment 8

Excessive bail
Cruel and unusual punishment

Amendment 9

People's rights

Amendment 10

State's rights

Amendments to the Constitution of the United States

1787	Constitution of the United States
1791	Bill of Rights
1795	11th Amendment – Citizen's cases against states
1804	12th Amendment – Electing the President and Vice President
1865	13th Amendment – Abolishing slavery
1868	14th Amendment – Citizenship, representation, broken oaths, Civil War debts
1870	15th Amendment – Voting rights for African Americans
1913	16th Amendment – Income tax
1913	17th Amendment – Direct election of senators
1919	18th Amendment – Prohibition
1920	19th Amendment – Voting rights for women
1933	20th Amendment – Start of terms for President and Congress, Temporary President
1933	21st Amendment – Repeal of prohibition
1951	22nd Amendment – Term limit for President
1961	23rd Amendment – Electoral vote for Washington D.C.
1964	24th Amendment – Poll taxes abolished
1967	25th Amendment – Presidential disability and succession
1971	26th Amendment – Voting rights for eighteen year olds
1992	27th Amendment – Congressional pay raises

Three Branches of Government

Executive

- President
- Vice President
- Cabinet Officers

Legislative

- House of Representatives
- Senate

Judicial

- Supreme Court
- Courts of Appeals
- Federal Courts

Legislative Branch

All Lawmaking Powers

Congress

Meets at least once a year, starting Jan. 3

House of Representatives

- ★ 435 Members
- ★ Based on population of each state
- ★ Must be at least 25 years old
- ★ U.S. Citizen for at least 7 years
- ★ Two year term in office
- ★ Can impeach officials
- ★ Leader is the Speaker of the House

Senate

- ★ 100 Members
- ★ 2 members for each state
- ★ Must be at least 30 years old
- ★ U.S. Citizen for at least 9 years
- ★ Six year term in office
- ★ Holds impeachment trials
- ★ Leader is the President of the Senate

How a Bill Becomes a law

House

Senate

A bill must pass in both houses then it is sent to the President.

If the President signs the bill or does nothing within 10 days then the bill becomes law.

If the President vetoes the bill, it returns to the house where it originated then goes to the other house.

Both houses have to pass the bill by a 2/3 majority to override the presidential veto.

Without a 2/3 majority the bill effectively dies.

With a 2/3 majority the bill becomes law.

Executive Departments

	Department of Agriculture (DOA) 1862	Secretary of Agriculture	The Department of Agriculture works to maintain or improve farm income. The department helps to expand markets for our agricultural products. The department works to stop poverty, malnutrition and hunger. The Department keeps our food supply safe.
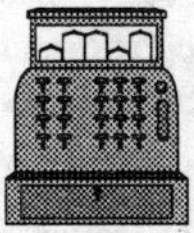	Department of Commerce (DOC) 1913	Secretary of Commerce	The Department of Commerce serves and promotes our country's international trade, economic growth and technological advancement. The Department grants patents and registers trademarks. The Department defines and keeps standards of weights and measures. The Department promotes travel and tourism. The Commerce Department includes the Bureau of the Census and the National Weather Service.
	Department of Defense (DOD) 1949	Secretary of Defense	The Department of Defense is responsible for providing the military forces needed to deter war and protect the security of our country. The Army, Navy, Air Force and Marine Corps are the branches of the military. The President is the Commander in Chief of the military.
	Department of Education 1979	Secretary of Education	The Department of Education establishes and administers federal education programs. The Department works to ensure access to education and to promote educational excellence.
	Department of Energy (DOE) 1977	Secretary of Energy	The Department of Energy works on our nation's energy policy. The Department is responsible for long term energy research and development. The Department generates and sells electricity. The Department is responsible for our nuclear weapons program.
	Department of Health and Human Services (HHS) 1953	Secretary of Health and Human Services	The Department of Health and Human Services is the department most involved with the people and the nation's human issues. The Department includes the Public Health Service, run by the Surgeon General. The department administers programs for health and welfare for everyone from newborn babies to the elderly. The Office for Civil Rights is in this Department.

	Department of Housing and Urban Development (HUD) 1965	Secretary of Housing and Urban Development	The Department of Housing and Urban Development is responsible for the nation's housing needs. The Department administers improvement and development programs for our nation's communities. The Department is responsible for fair housing opportunities.
	Department of the Interior 1849	Secretary of the Interior	The Department of the Interior is the nation's principal conservation agency. The Department is responsible for our country's public lands and natural resources. The Department manages our National Parks and National Forests. The Department includes the Bureau of Indian Affairs.
	Department of Justice 1870	Attorney General	The Department of Justice is the nation's largest law firm. The Department is responsible for protecting us from criminals, and subversion. The Department protects our free enterprise system. The Department of Justice represents the government in all legal cases.
	Department of Labor (DOL) 1913	Secretary of Labor	The Department of Labor promotes and develops workers in our country. The Department works to ensure safe working conditions and fair employment opportunities. The Department administers worker training and education programs.
	Department of State 1789	Secretary of State	The Department of State conducts our nation's foreign policy. The Department promotes and provides for our country's long-range security and well being. The Department protects U.S. citizens outside our country. The State Department negotiates treaties with foreign nations. The Department represents the U.S. in the United Nations.
	Department of Transportation (DOT) 1966	Secretary of Transportation	The Department of Transportation establishes and administers the nation's transportation policy. The Department plans, develops and constructs highways, railroads, airports, and urban mass transit.
	Department of the Treasury 1789	Secretary of the Treasury	The Department of the Treasury recommends economic, financial, tax and monetary policies. The Department enforces laws and protects the President. The Department prints money and mints coins. The Department manages the country's financial activities.

Department of Veterans Affairs (VA) 1989	Secretary of Veterans Affairs	The Department of Veterans Affairs administers programs which benefit veterans and their families. This includes compensation for disabilities or death, home loans, education, health care and rehabilitation.

Practice Questions

1. The introduction to the Constitution is called

   A. *pro tempore.*

   B. Article 1.

   C. the Preamble.

   D. the Bill of Rights.

2. The legislative body of the federal government is the

   A. President.

   B. Congress.

   C. Capitol.

   D. Supreme Court.

3. The number of Representatives each state has in the House is

   A. 435.

   B. two.

   C. based on population.

   D. three or less.

4. A Representative must be a resident of the state he or she represents and at least

   A. twenty-five years old.

   B. thirty years old.

   C. eighteen years old.

   D. thirty-five years old.

5. Representatives are elected to serve

   A. for life.

   B. two year terms.

   C. six year terms.

   D. four year terms.

6. The national count of the people which takes place every ten years is called the

   A. population.

   B. decade count.

   C. centennial.

   D. census.

7. The leader of the House is the

   A. President *pro tempore.*

   B. Vice President of the U.S.

   C. Secretary of State.

   D. Speaker.

8. The number of Senators representing each state is

   A. based on population.

   B. two.

   C. 100.

   D. at least one for every 30,000 people.

9. A Senator's term of office is

   A. six years.

   B. four years.

   C. life.

   D. two years.

10. A Senator must be a citizen of the U.S. for at least nine years and must be at least

   A. eighteen years old.

   B. twenty-five years old.

   C. thirty years old.

   D. thirty-five years old.

11. The leader of the Senate is called the

A. Speaker.

B. President.

C. Chief Justice.

D. *Pro Tempore.*

12. This leader is also the

A. Secretary of State.

B. leader of the House.

C. Vice President of the U.S.

D. head of the Supreme Court.

13. The only governmental body that can impeach an official is the

A. House.

B. Senate.

C. Supreme Court.

D. Cabinet.

14. The only governmental body that can hold an impeachment trial is the

A. House.

B. Senate.

C. Supreme Court.

D. Cabinet.

15. If found guilty in an impeachment trial, the harshest punishment an official can receive is

A. a prison sentence of not more than twenty years.

B. removal from office.

C. the death penalty.

D. probation.

16. Congress must meet at least once a year starting on

A. March 20.

B. the first Monday in December.

C. July 5.

D. January 3.

17. To expel a member of the House or Senate, at least this many members must agree:

A. three-fourths.

B. a simple majority.

C. two-thirds.

D. a majority plus the President.

18. The record of all that is said in House and Senate meetings is called the

A. Congressional Journal.

B. Minutes of Meetings Book.

C. Journal of Congressional Proceedings.

D. Congressional Record.

19. Senators and Representatives may not be punished for

A. felonies or breach of the peace.

B. what is said during their meetings.

C. impeachable offenses.

D. disorderly behavior.

20. All bills that deal with taxes must come from

A. the President.

B. the judicial branch.

C. the House.

D. the Senate.

21. To become a law, a bill must be signed by the President after passing both houses of Congress by

A. a two-thirds vote.

B. a simple majority vote.

C. a three-fourths vote.

D. the committees that worked on the bill.

22. If the President vetoes a bill, to become a law that bill must be repassed in both houses by

A. a two-thirds vote.

B. a simple majority vote.

C. a three-fourths vote.

D. the committees that worked on the bill.

23. Congress has the following powers except for

A. enforcing laws.

B. making money and deciding what it is worth.

C. declaring war.

D. borrowing money.

24. A law that punishes someone for something they did before that act became a crime is

A. a writ of habeus corpus.

B. a bill of attainder.

C. an ex post facto law.

D. an illegal incrimination law.

25. In the United States no one may be given a title

A. to federal property.

B. of nobility.

C. to a vehicle purchased in another country.

D. of prestige.

26. Without permission from Congress, states are not allowed to make agreements with

A. local municipalities.

B. individuals living within state boundaries.

C. the federal government.

D. other states or countries.

27. The executive branch of government

A. creates the laws.

B. judges the laws.

C. enforces the laws.

D. changes the laws.

28. The term of office for the President and Vice President is

A. two years.

B. four years.

C. six years.

D. life.

29. The President and Vice President are elected by

A. the popular vote of the people.

B. the Senate.

C. the Electoral College.

D. the political party conventions.

30. The President must be a natural born U.S. citizen and at least

A. eighteen years old.

B. twenty-five years old.

C. thirty years old.

D. thirty-five years old.

31. The President must take the oath of office swearing to

A. work cooperatively with the Congress.

B. defend the Constitution.

C. avoid going to war if possible.

D. work hard to keep all promises made during the campaign.

32. If two-thirds of the Senators present at a meeting agree, the President can

A. make treaties with other countries.

B. make laws dealing with executive department matters.

C. pardon officials who have been impeached.

D. make rules for the operation of the army and navy.

33. When the President speaks to Congress about the condition of the country it is called the

A. National Status address.

B. State of the Nation address.

C. State of the Union address.

D. Commander-in-Chief's address.

34. The leader of the Supreme Court is the

A. Commander-in-Chief.

B. Lead Justice.

C. Chief Justice.

D. President.

35. Supreme Court Justices have a term of office of

A. two years.

B. four years.

C. six years.

D. life.

36. The federal court system deals with all of the following types of cases except

A. disagreements between states.

B. the Constitution.

C. government treaties.

D. the breaking of state laws.

37. Except for impeachment trials, anyone accused of a crime has the right to

A. a trial by jury.

B. decide where the trial will take place.

C. request a specific judge hear the case.

D. be released from jail, before the trial, once bail has been paid.

38. To convict a person of treason, the person must confess in court or

A. the judge must find the defendant guilty.

B. all jury members must sign a letter of agreement with the verdict.

C. two witnesses must testify that they saw the act committed.

D. the judge must agree with the jury verdict of guilty.

39. All rules and regulations about federal lands are made by

A. Congress.

B. the Department of the Interior.

C. the executive branch of the federal government.

D. the state where the land is located.

40. The Constitution may be amended if

A. three-fourths of the state's legislatures agree.

B. two-thirds of both houses of Congress agree.

C. the President asks Congress to write an amendment.

D. the Governors of the states ask Congress to write an amendment.

41. If state laws conflict with the Constitution,

A. the state laws are followed.

B. the Constitution is followed.

C. Congress works out a compromise.

D. the President signs an executive order deciding the issue.

42. The Constitution was ratified on September 17,

A. 1912.

B. 1776.

C. 1787.

D. 1865.

43. The Bill of Rights

A. is Article VIII of the Constitution.

B. has been changed several times since it was first adopted.

C. gave the vote to women and African-Americans.

D. is the first ten amendments to the Constitution.

44. The First Amendment deals with freedom

A. of speech, religion and the press.

B. from unfair taxation.

C. for the slaves.

D. from unnecessary federal rules and regulations.

45. The Second Amendment guarantees people the right to

A. assemble and meet peacefully.

B. a fair and open trial in a court of law.

C. bear arms.

D. privacy and protection from search.

46. Amendment Three says people cannot be forced to

A. bear arms.

B. quarter soldiers in their homes.

C. incriminate themselves.

D. testify against members of their families.

47. The Fourth Amendment says people have the right to

A. be protected from illegal searches.

B. be protected from foreign invasion.

C. be protected by arming themselves.

D. be protected in cases of national disaster.

48. Amendment Five says no one can be forced

A. to testify against someone in their family.

B. to testify against themselves in court.

C. to answer questions posed by the judge.

D. to have a jury trial.

49. Amendment Six says a person accused of a crime has the right to

A. choose the members of the jury.

B. select the judge who will hear the case.

C. have a grand jury hear the case.

D. have an attorney represent him or her in court.

50. The Seventh Amendment says if a case involves more than twenty dollars

A. the defendant must reimburse the court costs if found guilty.

B. a speedy and public trial is guaranteed.

C. the people in the case may ask for a jury trial.

D. the jury must be composed of twelve to twenty-three people.

51. Amendment Eight says it is forbidden to require

A. defendants to hire their own attorneys.

B. excessive bail or fines.

C. witnesses to testify against defendants.

D. a jury trial.

52. Amendment Nine says

A. the people have many rights not listed in the Constitution.

B. no one may be forced to incriminate themselves.

C. judges may force witnesses to testify in court.

D. the government may not take private property without paying a fair price.

53. The Tenth Amendment says the states

A. and people have all the powers not given to the U.S. Government by the Constitution.

B. may choose electors to vote for presidential candidates in national elections.

C. may not go to war unless they are being attacked.

D. may not impose poll taxes or other taxes to keep people from voting.

54. The Eleventh Amendment says

A. states may not grant titles of nobility.

B. no one may give up United States citizenship.

C. federal courts won't hear cases brought against a state by people from other states or countries.

D. the people have many rights that are not listed in the Constitution.

55. The Twelfth Amendment says that if no candidate wins more than half of the electoral votes in a presidential election, the

A. Senate votes to elect the President.

B. House votes to elect the President.

C. states hold conventions to elect the President.

D. electors vote again to elect the President.

56. Amendment Thirteen to the Constitution

A. gave women the vote.

B. gave the vote to former slaves over the age of twenty-one.

C. says Confederate war debts will not be paid by the federal government.

D. abolished slavery.

57. The Fourteenth Amendment says that

A. state laws supersede federal laws.

B. states cannot take away rights of citizens.

C. states may collect income taxes from the people.

D. liquor is prohibited in the United States.

58. The Fifteenth Amendment

A. abolished slavery.

B. gave women the vote.

C. says no one can lose their right to vote simply because of the color of their skin.

D. gave the federal government the right to collect income taxes from citizens.

59. The Sixteenth Amendment gave Congress the power to

A. pay debts incurred by the Union during the Civil War.

B. collect income taxes from the people.

C. counteract presidential vetoes.

D. repeal prohibition.

60. The Seventeenth Amendment gave the people the right to

A. elect Senators.

B. change the term of office for Senators.

C. vote regardless of their skin color.

D. vote regardless of their gender.

61. The Eighteenth Amendment

A. abolished slavery.

B. prohibited the sale of alcohol.

C. changed the starting dates for governmental officer's terms of office to January.

D. gave women the right to vote.

62. The Nineteenth Amendment

A. prohibited the sale of alcohol.

B. repealed the amendment outlawing alcohol.

C. gave women the right to vote.

D. provides for an Acting President if the President-elect dies before taking office.

63. The Twentieth Amendment says

A. no state can impose poll taxes.

B. Congress may collect income taxes.

C. Prohibition is no longer federal law.

D. the President's term of office ends on January 20.

64. The Twenty-First Amendment

A. repeals Prohibition.

B. says the President's term ends on January 20.

C. gave women the right to vote.

D. gave eighteen year olds the right to vote.

65. The Twenty-Second Amendment

A. repeals Prohibition.

B. gives Congress the power to collect income taxes.

C. limits Presidential term of office to 10 years.

D. gave eighteen year olds the right to vote.

66. The Twenty-Third Amendment gave

A. eighteen year olds the right to vote.

B. women the right to vote.

C. the people of Washington, D.C. the right to choose presidential electors

D. the office of President a term limit of ten years.

67. The Twenty-Fourth Amendment says

A. the people of Washington, D.C. can choose presidential electors.

B. women have the right to vote.

C. eighteen year olds have the right to vote.

D. poll taxes cannot be used to keep people from voting.

68. Amendment Twenty-Five says

A. the Vice President may become President if the President is unable to do the job.

B. eighteen year olds have the right to vote.

C. the people of Washington, D.C. have the right to choose presidential electors.

D. no one may be kept from voting because they haven't paid a tax.

69. The Twenty-Sixth Amendment gives

A. the people of Washington, D.C. the right to choose presidential electors.

B. eighteen year olds the right to vote.

C. the Vice President the power to become the Acting President in time of national emergency.

D. women the right to vote.

70. The U.S. Constitution is composed of _____ articles and twenty-seven amendments.

A. 7

B. 9

C. 10

D. 27

Answers to Practice Questions

1. C	11. B	21. B	31. B	41. B	51. B	61. B
2. B	12. C	22. A	32. A	42. C	52. A	62. C
3. C	13. A	23. A	33. C	43. D	53. A	63. D
4. A	14. B	24. C	34. C	44. A	54. C	64. A
5. B	15. B	25. B	35. D	45. C	55. B	65. C
6. D	16. D	26. D	36. D	46. B	56. D	66. C
7. D	17. C	27. C	37. A	47. A	57. B	67. D
8. B	18. D	28. B	38. C	48. B	58. C	68. A
9. A	19. B	29. C	39. A	49. D	59. B	69. B
10. C	20. C	30. D	40. A	50. C	60. A	70. A

PREAMBLE

We, the people of the United States, in order to form a more perfect Union, establish justice, insure domestic tranquility, provide for the common defense, promote the general welfare, and secure the blessings of liberty to ourselves and our posterity do ordain and establish this Constitution for the United States of America.

ARTICLE I

Section 1

All legislative powers herein granted shall be vested in a Congress of the United States, which shall consist of a Senate and House of Representatives.

Section 2

The House of Representatives shall be composed of members chosen every second year by the people of the several States, and the electors in each State shall have the qualifications requisite for electors of the most numerous branch of the State Legislature.

No person shall be a Representative who shall not have attained to the age of twenty-five years, and been seven years a citizen of the United States, and who shall not, when elected, be an inhabitant of that State in which he shall be chosen.

[Representatives and direct taxes shall be apportioned among the several States which may be included within this Union, according to their respective numbers, which shall be determined by adding to the whole number of free persons, including those bound to service for a term of years, and excluding Indians not taxed, three-fifths of all other persons.][1] The actual enumeration shall be made within three years after the first meeting of the Congress of the United States, and within every subsequent term of ten years, in such manner as they shall by law direct. The number of Representatives shall not exceed one for every thirty thousand, but each State shall have at least one Representative; and until such enumeration shall be made, the State of New Hampshire shall be entitled to choose three, Massachusetts eight, Rhode Island and Providence Plantations one, Connecticut five, New York six, New Jersey four, Pennsylvania eight, Delaware one, Maryland six, Virginia ten, North Carolina five, South Carolina five, and Georgia three.

When vacancies happen in the representation from any State, the Executive Authority thereof shall issue writs of election to fill such vacancies.

The House of Representatives shall choose their Speaker and other officers; and shall have the sole power of impeachment.

Section 3

The Senate of the United States shall be composed of two Senators from each State, [chosen by the Legislature thereof,][2] for six years; and each Senator shall have one vote.

Immediately after they shall be assembled in consequence of the first election, they shall be divided as equally as may be into three classes. The seats of the Senators of the first class shall be vacated at the expiration of the second year, of the second class at the expiration of the fourth year, and of the third class at the expiration of the sixth year, so that one-third may be chosen every second year; [and if vacancies

---

[1] Changed by the 14th Amendment

[2] Changed by the 17th Amendment

happen by resignation, or otherwise, during the recess of the Legislature of any State, the Executive thereof may make temporary appointments until the next meeting of the Legislature, which shall then fill such vacancies.][3]

No person shall be a Senator who shall not have attained to the age of thirty years, and been nine years a citizen of the United States, and who shall not, when elected, be an inhabitant of that State for which he shall be chosen.

The Vice President of the United States shall be President of the Senate, but shall have no vote, unless they be equally divided.

The Senate shall choose their other officers, and also a President pro tempore, in the absence of the Vice President, or when he shall exercise the office of President of the United States.

The Senate shall have the sole power to try all impeachments. When sitting for that purpose, they shall be on oath or affirmation. When the President of the United States is tried, the Chief Justice shall preside: and no person shall be convicted without the concurrence of two-thirds of the members present.

Judgment in cases of impeachment shall not extend further than to removal from office, and disqualification to hold and enjoy any office of honor, trust or profit under the United States: but the party convicted shall nevertheless be liable and subject to indictment, trial, judgment and punishment, according to law.

Section 4

The times, places and manner of holding elections for Senators and Representatives, shall be prescribed in each State by the Legislature thereof; but the Congress may at

---

[3] Changed by the 17th Amendment

any time by law make or alter such regulations, except as to the places of choosing Senators.

The Congress shall assemble at least once in every year, and such meeting shall [be on the first Monday in December,][4] unless they shall by law appoint a different day.

Section 5

Each House shall be the judge of the elections, returns and qualifications of its own members, and a majority of each shall constitute a quorum to do business; but a smaller number may adjourn from day to day, and may be authorized to compel the attendance of absent members, in such manner, and under such penalties as each House may provide.

Each House may determine the rules of its proceedings, punish its members for disorderly behavior, and, with the concurrence of two-thirds, expel a member.

Each House shall keep a journal of its proceedings, and from time to time publish the same, excepting such parts as may in their judgment require secrecy; and the yeas and nays of the members of either House on any question shall, at the desire of one-fifth of those present, be entered on the journal.

Neither House, during the session of Congress, shall, without the consent of the other, adjourn for more than three days, nor to any other place than that in which the two Houses shall be sitting.

---

[4] Changed by the 20th Amendment

Section 6

The Senators and Representatives shall receive a compensation for their services, to be ascertained by law, and paid out of the Treasury of the United States. They shall in all cases, except treason, felony and breach of the peace, be privileged from arrest during their attendance at the session of their respective Houses, and in going to and returning from the same; and for any speech or debate in either House, they shall not be questioned in any other place.

No Senator or Representative shall, during the time for which he was elected, be appointed to any civil office under the authority of the United States, which shall have been created, or the emoluments whereof shall have been increased during such time; and no person holding any office under the United States, shall be a member of either House during his continuance in office.

Section 7

All bills for raising revenue shall originate in the House of Representatives; but the Senate may propose or concur with amendments as on other bills.

Every bill which shall have passed the House of Representatives and the Senate, shall, before it becomes a law, be presented to the President of the United States; if he approves he shall sign it, but if not he shall return it, with his objections to that House in which it shall have originated, who shall enter the objections at large on their journal, and proceed to reconsider it. If after such reconsideration two-thirds of that House shall agree to pass the bill, it shall be sent, together with the objections, to the other House, by which it shall likewise be reconsidered, and if approved by two-thirds of that House, it shall become a law. But in all such cases the votes of both Houses shall be determined by yeas and nays, and the names of the persons voting for and against the bill shall be entered on the journal of each House respectively. If any bill shall not be returned by the President within ten days (Sundays excepted) after it shall have been presented to him, the same shall be a law, in like manner as if he had signed it, unless the Congress by their adjournment prevent its return, in which case it shall not be a law.

Every order, resolution, or vote to which the concurrence of the Senate and House of Representatives may be necessary (except on a question of adjournment) shall be presented to the President of the United States; and before the same shall take effect, shall be approved by him, or being disapproved by him, shall be repassed by two-thirds of the Senate and House of Representatives, according to the rules and limitations prescribed in the case of a bill.

Section 8

The Congress shall have power

To lay and collect taxes, duties, imposts and excises, to pay the debts and provide for the common defense and general welfare of the United States; but all duties, imposts and excises shall be uniform throughout the United States;

To borrow money on the credit of the United States;

To regulate commerce with foreign nations, and among the several States, and with the Indian tribes;

To establish a uniform rule of naturalization, and uniform laws on the subject of bankruptcies throughout the United States;

To coin money, regulate the value thereof, and of foreign coin, and fix the standard of weights and measures;

To provide for the punishment of counterfeiting the securities and current coin of the United States;

To establish post-offices and post roads;

To promote the progress of science and useful arts, by securing for limited times to authors and inventors the exclusive right to their respective writings and discoveries;

To constitute tribunals inferior to the Supreme Court;

To define and punish piracies and felonies committed on the high seas, and offenses against the law of nations;

To declare war, grant letters of marque and reprisal, and make rules concerning captures on land and water;

To raise and support armies, but no appropriation of money to that use shall be for a longer term than two years;

To provide and maintain a navy;

To make rules for the government and regulation of the land and naval forces;

To provide for calling forth the militia to execute the laws of the Union, suppress insurrections and repel invasions;

To provide for organizing, arming, and disciplining the militia, and for governing such part of them as may be employed in the service of the United States, reserving to the States respectively, the appointment of the officers, and the authority of training the militia according to the discipline prescribed by Congress;

To exercise exclusive legislation in all cases whatsoever, over such district (not exceeding ten miles square) as may, by cession of particular States, and the acceptance of Congress, become the seat of the Government of the United States, and to exercise like authority over all places purchased by the consent of the Legislature of the State in which the same shall be, for the erection of forts, magazines, arsenals, dockyards, and other needful buildings;—And

To make all laws which shall be necessary and proper for carrying into execution the foregoing powers, and all other powers vested by this Constitution in the Government of the United States, or in any department or officer thereof.

Section 9

The migration or importation of such persons as any of the States now existing shall think proper to admit, shall not be prohibited by the Congress prior to the year one thousand eight hundred and eight, but a tax or duty may be imposed on such importation, not exceeding ten dollars for each person.

The privilege of the writ of habeas corpus shall not be suspended, unless when in cases of rebellion or invasion the public safety may require it.

No bill of attainder or ex post facto law shall be passed.

[No capitation, or other direct, tax shall be laid, unless in proportion to the census or enumeration herein before directed to be taken.][5]

No tax or duty shall be laid on articles exported from any State.

No preference shall be given by any regulation of commerce or revenue to the ports of one State over those of another: nor shall vessels bound to, or from, one State, be obliged to enter, clear, or pay duties in another.

No money shall be drawn from the Treasury, but in consequence of appropriations made by law; and a regular statement and account of the receipts and expenditures of all public money shall be published from time to time.

---

[5] Changed by the 16th Amendment

No title of nobility shall be granted by the United States: and no person holding any office of profit or trust under them, shall, without the consent of the Congress, accept of any present, emolument, office, or title, of any kind whatever, from any king, prince, or foreign state.

Section 10

No State shall enter into any treaty, alliance, or confederation; grant letters of marque and reprisal; coin money; emit bills of credit; make anything but gold and silver coin a tender in payment of debts; pass any bill of attainder, ex post facto law, or law impairing the obligation of contracts, or grant any title of nobility.

No State shall, without the consent of the Congress, lay any imposts or duties on imports or exports, except what may be absolutely necessary for executing its inspection laws: and the net produce of all duties and imposts, laid by any State on imports or exports, shall be for the use of the Treasury of the United States; and all such laws shall be subject to the revision and control of the Congress.

No State shall, without the consent of Congress, lay any duty of tonnage, keep troops, or ships of war in time of peace, enter into any agreement or compact with another State, or with a foreign power, or engage in war, unless actually invaded, or in such imminent danger as will not admit of delay.

ARTICLE II

Section 1

The Executive power shall be vested in a President of the United States of America. He shall hold his office during the term of four years, and together with the Vice President, chosen for the same term, be elected as follows

Each State shall appoint, in such manner as the Legislature thereof may direct, a number of electors, equal to the whole number of Senators and Representatives to which the State may be entitled in the Congress: but no Senator or Representative, or person holding an office of trust or profit under the United States shall be appointed an elector.

[The electors shall meet in their respective States, and vote ballot for two persons, of whom one at least shall not be an inhabitant of the same State with themselves. And they shall make a list of all the persons voted for, and of the number of votes for each; which list they shall sign and certify, and transmit sealed to the seat of the Government of the United States, directed to the President of the Senate. The President of the Senate shall, in the presence of the Senate and House of Representatives, open all the certificates, and the votes shall then be counted. The person having the greatest number of votes shall be the President, if such number be a majority of the whole number of electors appointed; and if there be more than one who have such majority, and have an equal number of votes, then the House of Representatives shall immediately choose by ballot one of them for President; and if no person have a majority, then from the five highest on the list the said House shall in like manner choose the President. But in choosing the President, the votes shall be taken by States, the representation from each State having one vote; a quorum for this purpose shall consist of a member or members from two-thirds of the States, and a majority of all the States shall be necessary to a choice. In every case, after the choice of the President, the person having the greatest number of votes of the electors shall be the Vice President. But if there should remain two or more who have equal votes, the Senate shall choose from them by ballot the Vice President.][6]

The Congress may determine the time of choosing the electors, and the day on which they shall give their votes; which day shall be the same throughout the United States.

---

[6] Changed By the 12th Amendment

No person except a natural born citizen, or a citizen of the United States, at the time of the adoption of this Constitution, shall be eligible to the office of President; neither shall any person be eligible to that office who shall not have attained to the age of thirty-five years, and been fourteen years a resident within the United States.

[In case of the removal of the President from office, or of his death, resignation, or inability to discharge the powers and duties of the said office, the same shall devolve on the Vice President, and the Congress may by law provide for the case of removal, death, resignation or inability, both of the President and Vice President, declaring what officer shall then act as President, and such officer shall act accordingly, until the disability be removed, or a President shall be elected.][7]

The President shall, at stated times, receive for his services, a compensation, which shall neither be increased nor diminished during the period for which he shall have been elected, and he shall not receive within that period any other emolument from the United States, or any of them.

Before he enter on the execution of his office, he shall take the following oath or affirmation: "I do solemnly swear (or affirm) that I will faithfully execute the office of President of the United States, and will to the best of my ability, preserve, protect and defend the Constitution of the United States."

Section 2

The President shall be Commander-in-Chief of the Army and Navy of the United States, and of the militia of the several States, when called into the actual service of the United States; he may require the opinion, in writing, of the principal officer in each of the executive departments, upon any subject relating to the duties of their

---

[7] Changed by the 20th and 25th Amendment

respective offices, and he shall have power to grant reprieves and pardons for offenses against the United States, except in cases of impeachment.

He shall have power, by and with the advice and consent of the Senate, to make treaties, provided two-thirds of the Senators present concur; and he shall nominate, and by and with the advice and consent of the Senate, shall appoint ambassadors, other public ministers and consuls, judges of the Supreme Court, and all other officers of the United States, whose appointments are not herein otherwise provided for, and which shall be established by law: but the Congress may by law vest the appointment of such inferior officers, as they think proper, in the President alone, in the courts of law, or in the heads of departments.

The President shall have power to fill up all vacancies that may happen during the recess of the Senate, by granting commissions, which shall expire at the end of their next session.

Section 3

He shall from time to time give to the Congress information of the state of the Union, and recommend to their consideration such measures as he shall judge necessary and expedient; he may, on extraordinary occasions, convene both Houses, or either of them, and in case of disagreement between them, with respect to the time of adjournment, he may adjourn them to such time as he shall think proper; he shall receive ambassadors and other public ministers; he shall take care that the laws be faithfully executed, and shall commission all the officers of the United States.

Section 4

The President, Vice President, and all civil officers of the United States, shall be removed from office on impeachment for, and conviction of, treason, bribery, or other high crimes and misdemeanors.

ARTICLE III

Section 1

The judicial power of the United States, shall be vested in one Supreme Court, and in such inferior courts as the Congress may from time to time ordain and establish. The judges, both of the Supreme and inferior courts, shall hold their offices during good behavior, and shall at stated times, receive for their services, a compensation, which shall not be diminished during their continuance in office.

Section 2

The judicial power shall extend to all cases, in law and equity, arising under this Constitution, the laws of the United States, and treaties made, or which shall be made, under their authority; to all cases affecting ambassadors, other public ministers and consuls; to all cases of admiralty and maritime jurisdiction; to controversies to which the United States shall be a party; to controversies between two or more States; [between a State and citizens of another State;][8] between citizens of different States, between citizens of the same State claiming lands under grants of different States, [and between a State, or the citizens thereof, and foreign states, citizens or subjects.][9]

In all cases affecting ambassadors, other public ministers and consuls, and those in which a State shall be party, the Supreme Court shall have original jurisdiction. In all the other cases before mentioned, the Supreme Court shall have appellate

---

[8] Changed by the 11th Amendment

[9] Changed by the 11th Amendment

jurisdiction, both as to law and fact, with such exceptions, and under such regulations as the Congress shall make.

The trial of all crimes, except in cases of impeachment, shall be by jury; and such trial shall be held in the State where the said crimes shall have been committed; but when not committed within any State, the trial shall be at such place or places as the Congress may by law have directed.

Section 3

Treason against the United States, shall consist only in levying war against them, or in adhering to their enemies, giving them aid and comfort. No person shall be convicted of treason unless on the testimony of two witnesses to the same overt act, or on confession in open court.

The Congress shall have power to declare the punishment of treason, but no attainder of treason shall work corruption of blood, or forfeiture except during the life of the person attainted.

ARTICLE IV

Section 1

Full faith and credit shall be given in each State to the public acts, records, and judicial proceedings of every other State. And the Congress may by general laws prescribe the manner in which such acts, records and proceedings shall be proved, and the effect thereof.

Section 2

The citizens of each State shall be entitled to all privileges and immunities of citizens in the several States.

A person charged in any State with treason, felony, or other crime, who shall flee from justice, and be found in another State, shall on demand of the Executive authority of the State from which he fled, be delivered up, to be removed to the State having jurisdiction of the crime.

No person held to service or labor in one State, under the laws thereof, escaping into another, shall in consequence of any law or regulation therein, be discharged from such service or labor, but shall be delivered up on claim of the party to whom such service or labor may be due.][10]

Section 3

New States may be admitted by the Congress into this Union; but no new State shall be formed or erected within the jurisdiction of any other State; nor any State be formed by the junction of two or more States, or parts of States, without the consent of the Legislatures of the States concerned as well as of the Congress.

The Congress shall have power to dispose of and make all needful rules and regulations respecting the territory or other property belonging to the United States; and nothing in this Constitution shall be so construed as to prejudice any claims of the United States, or of any particular State.

Section 4

The United States shall guarantee to every State in this Union a Republican form of government, and shall protect each of them against invasion; and on application of the Legislature, or of the Executive (when the Legislature cannot be convened) against domestic violence.

---

[10] Changed by the 13th Amendment

ARTICLE V

The Congress, whenever two-thirds of both Houses shall deem it necessary, shall propose amendments to this Constitution, or, on the application of the Legislatures of two-thirds of the several States, shall call a convention for proposing amendments, which, in either case, shall be valid to all intents and purposes, as part of this Constitution, when ratified by the Legislatures of three-fourths of the several States, or by conventions in three-fourths thereof, as the one or the other mode of ratification may be proposed by the Congress; provided that no amendment which may be made prior to the year one thousand eight hundred and eight shall in any manner affect the first and fourth clauses in the Ninth Section of the First Article; and that no State, without its consent, shall be deprived of its equal suffrage in the Senate.

ARTICLE VI

All debts contracted and engagements entered into, before the adoption of this Constitution, shall be as valid against the United States under this Constitution, as under the Confederation.

This Constitution, and the laws of the United States which shall be made in pursuance thereof; and all treaties made, or which shall be made, under the authority of the United States, shall be the supreme law of the land; and the judges in every State shall be bound thereby, any thing in the Constitution or laws of any State to the contrary notwithstanding.

The Senators and Representatives before mentioned, and the members of the several State Legislatures, and all executive and judicial officers, both of the United States and of the several States, shall be bound by oath or affirmation, to support this Constitution; but no religious test shall ever be required as a qualification to any office or public trust under the United States.

ARTICLE VII

The ratification of the Conventions of nine States, shall be sufficient for the establishment of this Constitution between the States so ratifying the same.

Done in convention by the unanimous consent of the States present the Seventeenth day of September in the year of our Lord one thousand seven hundred and eighty seven, and of the independence of the United States of America the Twelfth. In witness whereof we have hereunto subscribed our names.

George Washington, President and deputy from Virginia.

New Hampshire	John Langdon, Nicholas Gilman.
Massachusetts	Nathaniel Gorham, Rufus King.
Connecticut	Wm. Saml. Johnson, Roger Sherman.
New York	Alexander Hamilton.
New Jersey	Wil: Livingston, David Brearley, Wm. Paterson, Jona: Dayton.
Pennsylvania	B. Franklin, Thomas Mifflin, Robt. Morris, Geo. Clymer, Thos. FitzSimons, Jared Ingersoll, James Wilson, Gouv. Morris.
Delaware	Geo: Read, Gunning Bedford Jun., John Dickinson, Richard Bassett, Jaco: Broom.
Maryland	James McHenry, Daniel of Saint Thomas' Jenifer, Danl. Carroll.
Virginia	John Blair, James Madison Jr.
North Carolina	Wm. Blount, Rich'd. Dobbs Spaight, Hugh Williamson.
South Carolina	J. Rutledge, Charles Cotesworth Pinckney, Charles Pinckney, Pierce Butler.
Georgia	William Few, Abr. Baldwin.

Attest William Jackson Secretary.

Bill of Rights

AMENDMENT I

Congress shall make no law respecting an establishment of religion, or prohibiting the free exercise thereof; or abridging the freedom of speech, or of the press; or the right of the people peaceably to assemble, and to petition the Government for a redress of grievances.

AMENDMENT II

A well-regulated militia, being necessary to the security of a free State, the right of the people to keep and bear arms, shall not be infringed.

AMENDMENT III

No soldier shall, in time of peace be quartered in any house, without the consent of the owner, nor in time of war, but in a manner to be prescribed by law.

AMENDMENT IV

The right of the people to be secure in their persons, houses, papers, and effects, against unreasonable searches and seizures, shall not be violated, and no warrants shall issue, but upon probable cause, supported by oath or affirmation, and particularly describing the place to be searched, and the persons or things to be seized.

AMENDMENT IV

The right of the people to be secure in their persons, houses, papers, and effects, against unreasonable searches and seizures, shall not be violated, and no warrants shall issue, but upon probable cause, supported by oath or affirmation, and particularly describing the place to be searched, and the persons or things to be seized.

AMENDMENT V

No person shall be held to answer for a capital, or otherwise infamous crime, unless on a presentment or indictment of a Grand Jury, except in cases arising in the land or naval forces, or in the militia, when in actual service in time of war or public danger; nor shall any person be subject for the same offense to be twice put in jeopardy of life or limb; nor shall be compelled in any criminal case to be a witness against himself, nor be deprived of life, liberty, or property, without due process of law; nor shall private property be taken for public use without just compensation.

AMENDMENT VI

In all criminal prosecutions, the accused shall enjoy the right to a speedy and public trial, by an impartial jury of the State and district wherein the crime shall have been committed, which district shall have been previously ascertained by law, and to be informed of the nature and cause of the accusation; to be confronted with the witnesses against him; to have compulsory process for obtaining witnesses in his favor, and to have the assistance of counsel for his defense.

AMENDMENT VII

In suits at common law, where the value in controversy shall exceed twenty dollars, the right of trial by jury shall be preserved, and no fact tried by a jury shall be otherwise reexamined in any court of the United States, than according to the rules of the common law.

AMENDMENT VIII

Excessive bail shall not be required, nor excessive fines imposed, nor cruel and unusual punishments inflicted.

AMENDMENT IX

The enumeration in the Constitution, of certain rights, shall not be construed to deny or disparage others retained by the people.

AMENDMENT X

The powers not delegated to the United States by the Constitution, nor prohibited by it to the States, are reserved to the States respectively, or to the people.

Amendments to the Constitution

AMENDMENT XI

(Ratified February 7, 1795)

The judicial power of the United States shall not be construed to extend to any suit in law or equity, commenced or prosecuted against one of the United States by citizens of another State, or by citizens or subjects of any foreign state.

AMENDMENT XII

(Ratified June 15, 1804)

The Electors shall meet in their respective States and vote by ballot for President and Vice-President, one of whom, at least, shall not be an inhabitant of the same State with themselves; they shall name in their ballots the person voted for as President, and in distinct ballots the person voted for as Vice-President, and they shall make distinct lists of all persons voted for as President, and of all persons voted for as Vice-President, and of the number of votes for each, which lists they shall sign and certify, and transmit sealed to the seat of the Government of the United States, directed to the President of the Senate; the President of the Senate shall, in the presence of the Senate and House of Representatives, open all the certificates and the votes shall then be counted;—The person having the greatest number of votes for President, shall be the President, if such number be a majority of the whole number of Electors appointed; and if no person have such majority, then from the persons having the highest numbers not exceeding three on the list of those voted for as President, the House of Representatives shall choose immediately, by ballot, the President. But in choosing the President, the votes shall be taken by States, the representation from each State having one vote; a quorum for this purpose shall consist of a member or members from two-thirds of the States, and a majority of all the States shall be necessary to a choice. [And if the House of Representatives shall not choose a President whenever the right of choice shall devolve upon them, before the fourth day of March next following, then the Vice-President shall act as President, as in the case of the death or other constitutional disability of the President.][11] The person having the greatest number of votes as Vice-President, shall be the Vice-President, if such number be a majority of the whole number of Electors appointed, and if no person have a majority, then from the two highest numbers on the list, the Senate shall choose the Vice-President; a quorum for the purpose shall consist of two-thirds of the whole number of Senators, and a majority of the whole number shall be necessary to a choice. But no person constitutionally ineligible to the office of President shall be eligible to that of Vice-President of the United States.

AMENDMENT XIII

(Ratified December 6, 1868)

Section 1.

Neither slavery nor involuntary servitude, except as a punishment for crime whereof the party shall have been duly convicted, shall exist within the United States or any place subject to their jurisdiction.

Section 2

Congress shall have power to enforce this article by appropriate legislation.

---

[11] Changed by the 20th Amendment

AMENDMENT XIV

(Ratified July 9, 1868)

Section 1.

All persons born or naturalized in the United States, and subject to the jurisdiction thereof, are citizens of the United States and of the State wherein they reside. No State shall make or enforce any law which shall abridge the privileges or immunities of citizens of the United States; nor shall any State deprive any person of life, liberty, or property, without due process of law; nor deny to any person within its jurisdiction the equal protection of the laws.

Section 2.

Representatives shall be apportioned among the several States according to their respective numbers, counting the whole number of persons in each State, excluding Indians not taxed. But when the right to vote at any election for the choice of Electors for President and Vice-President of the United States, Representatives in Congress, the executive and judicial officers of a State, or the members of the Legislature thereof, is denied to any of the male inhabitants of such State, being twenty-one years of age, and, citizens of the United States, or in any way abridged, except for participation in rebellion, or other crime, the basis of representation therein shall be reduced in the proportion which the number of such male citizens shall bear to the whole number of male citizens twenty-one years of age in such State.

Section 3.

No person shall be a Senator or Representative in Congress, or Elector of President and Vice-President, or hold any office, civil or military, under the United States, or under any State, who, having previously taken an oath, as a member of Congress, or as an officer of the United States, or as a member of any State Legislature, or as an executive or judicial officer of any State, to support the Constitution of the United States, shall have engaged in insurrection or rebellion against the same, or given aid or comfort to the enemies thereof. But Congress may by a vote of two-thirds of each House, remove such disability.

Section 4.

The validity of the public debt of the United States, authorized by law, including debts incurred for payment of pensions and bounties for services in suppressing insurrection or rebellion, shall not be questioned. But neither the United States nor any State shall assume or pay any debt or obligation incurred in aid of insurrection or rebellion against the United States, or any claim for the loss or emancipation of any slave; but all such debts, obligations and claims, shall be held illegal and void.

Section 5.

The Congress shall have power to enforce, by appropriate legislation, the provisions of this article.

AMENDMENT XV

(Ratified February 3, 1870)

Section 1.

The right of citizens of the United States to vote shall not be denied or abridged by the United States or by any State on account of race, color, or previous condition of servitude.

Section 2.

The Congress shall have power to enforce this article by appropriate legislation.

AMENDMENT XVI

(Ratified February 3, 1913)

The Congress shall have power to lay and collect taxes on incomes, from whatever source derived, without apportionment among the several States, and without regard to any census or enumeration.

AMENDMENT XVII

(Ratified April 8, 1913)

The Senate of the United States shall be composed of two Senators from each State, elected by the people thereof, for six years; and each Senator shall have one vote. The electors in each State shall have the qualifications requisite for electors of the most numerous branch of the State Legislatures.

When vacancies happen in the representation of any State in the Senate, the executive authority of such State shall issue writs of election to fill such vacancies: Provided, That the Legislature of any State may empower the Executive thereof to make temporary appointments until the people fill the vacancies by election as the Legislature may direct.

This amendment shall not be so construed as to affect the election or term of any Senator chosen before it becomes valid as part of the Constitution.

AMENDMENT XVIII

(Ratified January 16, 1919)[12]

Section 1.

After one year from the ratification of this article the manufacture, sale, or transportation of intoxicating liquors within, the importation thereof into, or the exportation thereof from the United States and all territory subject to the jurisdiction thereof for beverage purposes is hereby prohibited.

Section 2.

The Congress and the several States shall have concurrent power to enforce this article by appropriate legislation.

Section 3.

This article shall be inoperative unless it shall have been ratified as an amendment to the Constitution by the Legislatures of the several States, as provided in the

---

[12] Repealed by the 21st Amendment, December 5, 1933

Constitution, within seven years from the date of the submission hereof to the States by the Congress.)

AMENDMENT XIX

(Ratified August 18, 1920)

The right of citizens of the United States to vote shall not be denied or abridged by the United States or by any State on account of sex.

Congress shall have power to enforce this Article by appropriate legislation.

AMENDMENT XX

(Ratified January 23, 1933)

Section 1.

The terms of the President and Vice President shall end at noon on the 20th day of January, and the terms of Senators and Representatives at noon on the 3rd day of January, of the years in which such terms would have ended if this article had not been ratified; and the terms of their successors shall then begin.

Section 2.

The Congress shall assemble at least once in every year, and such meeting shall begin at noon on the 3rd day of January, unless they shall by law appoint a different day.

Section 3.

If, at the time fixed for the beginning of the term of the President, the President elect shall have died, the Vice President elect shall become President. If a President shall not have been chosen before the time fixed for the beginning of his term, or if the President elect shall have failed to qualify, then the Vice President elect shall act as President until a President shall have qualified; and the Congress may by law provide for the case wherein neither a President elect nor a Vice President elect shall have qualified, declaring who shall then act as President, or the manner in which one who is to act shall be selected, and such person shall act accordingly until a President or Vice President shall have qualified.

Section 4.

The Congress may by law provide for the case of the death of any of the persons from whom the House of Representatives may choose a President whenever the right of choice shall have devolved upon them, and for the case of the death of any of the persons from whom the Senate may choose a Vice President whenever the right of choice shall have devolved upon them.

Section 5.

Sections 1 and 2 shall take effect on the 15th day of October following the ratification of this article.

Section 6.

This article shall be inoperative unless it shall have been ratified as an amendment to the Constitution by the Legislatures of three-fourths of the several States within seven years from the date of its submission.

AMENDMENT XXI

(Ratified December 5, 1933)

Section 1.

The eighteenth article of amendment to the Constitution of the United States is hereby repealed.

Section 2.

The transportation or importation into any State, Territory, or Possession of the United States for delivery or use therein of intoxicating liquors, in violation of the laws thereof, is hereby prohibited.

Section 3.

This article shall be inoperative unless it shall have been ratified as an amendment to the Constitution by conventions in the several States, as provided in the Constitution, within seven years from the date of the submission hereof to the States by the Congress.

AMENDMENT XXII

(Ratified February 27, 1951)

Section 1.

No person shall be elected to the office of the President more than twice, and no person who has held the office of President, or acted as President, for more than two years of a term to which some other person was elected President shall be elected to the office of the President more than once. But this Article shall not apply to any person holding the office of President when this Article was proposed by the Congress, and shall not prevent any person who may be holding the office of President, or acting as President, during the term within which this Article becomes operative from holding the office of President or acting as President during the remainder of such term.

Section 2.

This article shall be inoperative unless it shall have been ratified as an amendment to the Constitution by the Legislatures of three-fourths of the several States within seven years from the date of its submission to the States by the Congress.

AMENDMENT XXIII

(Ratified March 29, 1961)

Section 1.

The District constituting the seat of Government of the United States shall appoint in such manner as the Congress may direct:

A number of electors of President and Vice President equal to the whole number of Senators and Representatives in Congress to which the District would be entitled if it were a State, but in no event more than the least populous State; they shall be in addition to those appointed by the States, but they shall be considered, for the purposes of the election of President and Vice President, to be electors appointed by a State; and they shall meet in the District and perform such duties as provided by the twelfth article of amendment.

Section 2.

The Congress shall have power to enforce this article by appropriate legislation.

AMENDMENT XXIV

(Ratified January 23, 1964)

Section 1.

The right of citizens of the United States to vote in any primary or other election for President or Vice President, for electors for President or Vice President, or for Senator or Representative in Congress, shall not be denied or abridged by the United States or any State by reason of failure to pay any poll tax or other tax.

Section 2.

The Congress shall have power to enforce this article by appropriate legislation.

AMENDMENT XXV

(Ratified February 10, 1967)

Section 1.

In case of the removal of the President from office or of his death or resignation, the Vice President shall become President.

Section 2.

Whenever there is a vacancy in the office of the Vice President, the President shall nominate a Vice President who shall take office upon confirmation by a majority vote of both houses of Congress.

Section 3.

Whenever the President transmits to the President pro tempore of the Senate and the Speaker of the House of Representatives his written declaration that he is unable to discharge the powers and duties of his office, and until he transmits to them a written declaration to the contrary, such powers and duties shall be discharged by the Vice President as Acting President.

Section 4.

Whenever the Vice President and a majority of either the principal officers of the executive departments or of such other body as Congress may by law provide, transmit to the President pro tempore of the Senate and the Speaker of the House of Representatives their written declaration that the President is unable to discharge the powers and duties of his office, the Vice President shall immediately assume the powers and duties of the office as Acting President.

Thereafter, when the President transmits to the President pro tempore of the Senate and the Speaker of the House of Representatives his written declaration that no inability exists, he shall resume the powers and duties of his office unless the Vice President and a majority of either the principal officers of the executive department or of such other body as Congress may by law provide, transmit within four days to the President pro tempore of the Senate and the Speaker of the House of Representatives their written declaration that the President is unable to discharge the powers and duties of his office. Thereupon Congress shall decide the issue, assembling within forty-eight hours for that purpose if not in session. If the Congress, within twenty-one days after receipt of the latter written declaration, or, if Congress is not in session, within twenty-one days after Congress is required to assemble, determines by two-thirds vote of both houses that the President is unable to discharge the powers and duties of his office, the Vice President shall continue to discharge the same as Acting President; otherwise, the President shall resume the powers and duties of his office.

AMENDMENT XXVI

(Ratified July 1, 1971)

Section 1.

The right of citizens of the United States, who are 18 years of age or older, to vote shall not be denied or abridged by the United States or any state on account of age.

Section 2.

The Congress shall have the power to enforce this article by appropriate legislation.

AMENDMENT XXVII

(Ratified May 7, 1992)

No law, varying the compensation for the services of the Senators and Representatives, shall take effect, until an election of Representatives shall have intervened.